AF488158

To ___________________________

Love ___________________________

"There is no influence so powerful as that of the mother."

- Sara Joseph Hale

Mom, Because Of You...

Written by Sonia Gomez-Neri

Illustrated by Mariia Luzina

Mary's Press

San Diego, California
Copyright © 2023
All rights reserved.
No part of this book may be reproduced
or transmitted in any form or by any means, electronic or
mechanical, including photocopying, recording or by any
information storage and retrieval system, without written
permission from the author, except for the inclusion of brief
quotations embodied in critical articles and reviews.

ISBN 979-8-9860669-8-1

"She is clothed with strength and dignity; she can laugh at the days to come. She speaks with wisdom, and faithful instruction is on her tongue."

Proverbs 31: 25-26

To my loving mother, Maria Elena Gomez, with utmost gratitude for all the valuable lessons you have taught me. I am the woman I am because of the impression you've made upon my soul. Your love has made me a better person in more ways than I can enumerate and now I pass along your lessons to my children. With all the love in my heart that springs from your well, I dedicate this book to you.

Sonia Gomez-Neri

To my mother Tetyana Luzina and my grandmother Lybov' Taran, who are far away from me right now but always in my heart.

Mariia Luzina

Mom, because of you...

compassion resides within my heart.

Because

of

you,

my inner strength refuses to depart.

Because of you,

loyalty keeps me steadfast and true.

Because

of

you,

integrity is the road that I choose.

Because of you,

family is what

matters most to

me.

Because of you,
I love with my heart's entirety.

Mom, because
of you I am...

Stronger

LESSON PLAN

Wiser

Happier

Playful

Faithful

And a mom,

Just like you.

My grandmother,
Isabel García Cavazos

My mother,
Maria Elena Gómez

My sister,
Laura Esparza

Thank you to the special mothers who have had the greatest impact on my life and who continue to inspire me to be a better person.

Blessed Mother Mary

About the Author

Sonia Gomez-Neri is a mother of four, godmother, wife, teacher, dog lover and devout Catholic. Along with writing, she enjoys running, indoor cycling, golfing, playing on her keyboard and cheering wildly at her kids' sporting events. She believes that being a mom is her greatest blessing.

She lives in San Diego, California.

About the Artist

Mariia Luzina was born in 1994, in the small town of Kryvyj Rih, Ukraine, where she lived with her grandparents. At the age of 15 she immigrated to Italy to live with her mother, where she obtained a degree in Political Science. From a young age Mariia loved to draw, but it was just a hobby, untill her best friend encouraged her to become an illustrator for children's books and once Mariia decided to give it a try, she never looked back!

Thank you

www.ingramcontent.com/pod-product-compliance
Lightning Source LLC
Chambersburg PA
CBHW041729100726
47973CB00010B/156